Surely, You Have Thought of This

A book about Life

Terry Page

Dunn Deal Publishing

copyright @ 2009 Terry Page
All rights reserved.

ISBN: 0-9819007-2-0
ISBN-13: 9780981900728

Visit www.booksurge.com to order additional copies.

Dedication

Dedicated to the Unborn &
To Climmer Lee Page, to whom I mourn
My niece Alexis who is a sweetheart
And a real blessing from the start
To those wishing to live the dream
Success can be yours once you
Believe in your team

SPEAKING OF BUSINESS

Broadcast TV

Trying to figure out why the viewer is frustrated today
Should be an easy task one must say
The same formula has been going on for years
The outcome is either going to be jeers or cheers.
Look at that TV station one Exec may shout
They have a program we don't carry, we may lose clout
If we think of a concept of our own
We may find ourselves alone
We must do as they do
Or the viewer won't have a clue
But sometimes I don't understand
Why the viewer isn't always our fan
They may watch other forms of
entertainment outside our broadcast
After all we have done for them they
appear to be leaving very fast
But look at radio, its lifespan has been long
They do it by playing the same old song
We will do it too by keeping our program variation few
Roll em but for heavens sake make sure
the camera has the same view
We can't take the chance of having drastic change
If the other station varies make sure we are in range
Just like our newscast all of the stories must be alike
Perhaps this ratings period our numbers will see a spike
We only show what the viewer wants to see
It is at no cost to them but to our advertisers there is a fee
There is no difference if you buy or not the cost is the same
Since the beginning of TV this is how we play the game
Never fear, there is no originality here
If you deviate we will steal your idea
Have the shows in the same increment
We will keep our schedule locked in cement
This holds true until the viewer alters
his schedule for next season

Then we move his favorite program for no apparent reason
Then the viewership for that show begins to decline
Our ratings fall further behind
We are not sure what went wrong, it worked last time
Let's cancel the show and see what else we can find
It's not possible we are doing anything incorrectly
We will blame the entire ordeal on the F.C.C.
It's their fault these other mediums are coming around
It was better for people when it was only us to be found
Sooner or later the viewer will return
because he has no clue
It will be just like one of our movies, Part 1 & Part II
Until that time we will recycle the same old idea
While all the time wonder why our future is unclear

Corporate America

Why can't we just be together
You want me there any kind of weather
Promises were made when we met
I had it made, I'll never forget
The wheels of Corporate will churn
Consumers it appears have money to burn
I made you money for advertising and expansion
The CEO dresses slick, & lives in a mansion
Leave for lunch now the place will be packed
Leave later I will receive much flack
You say believe in this fine institution
The GM used company dollars for prostitution
Come to work everyday let us do as we please
Tomorrow we will send your job overseas
You seem very negative we only want to speak
You came to us, it was a position you seek
We need two weeks if you plan to resign
But leave today, that will be just fine
Without you we won't fall behind
The secret to success we will never say
Be like us and do it today
Much time was spent for us to grow
Now look, today you must go
It is a pity you didn't figure it out
Because today, you could have much clout

Land of Opportunity

Visitors of the earth don't understand
There is a lie laid out on the land
Or perhaps just a misconception
Something about the right to bear weapons
But they shouldn't imply
Words of freedom are a lie
Those who laugh have money
Poverty to them must be funny
People with money have the influence
To the wealthy it all makes sense
Get a grip you have no rights
It is with your neighbor whom you fight
You kill each other while casting blame
On the problem you fuel the flame
All Men are created equal
American History we write the sequel
It sounds great but isn't correct
The rich have the true affect
The power we do have we squander
Our decision making ability you must wonder
Rulers are put in charge to help themselves
Their goal is to put our freedom on shelves
Any remaining tax exemption will be gone
The changes are coming it won't take long
Remember we left England to avoid the tax
Those early Brits certainly knew the facts
Get up! Stand to your feet
Don't be out done by a cheat
Many lost their lives for signing that sheet
Families were tortured, homes were burned
Come alive! Let's see what you've learned
When mistakes are made those rulers leave
Let's see what this generation can achieve
The foundation is there but the top in question
One day it may come down to combustion

Confidence moves on in the ranks
To the early settlers we should give thanks
Some of the reasoning we draw a blank
So long ago many may think
Luckily certain ships didn't sink
Back then they had a good reason
Difference is, they called it treason

Mad Employee

I don't understand why you treat me this way
When I first began here you said I could stay
Now I hear in the news my job is going away
My office is so big with a nice window and oh so plush
Now I find out it is my job you are going to flush
The good times we had as I cashed my giant checks
This day of ruin is crazy; it's all just too complex
The news reports there were errors
made by upper management
Issues arrived that the company could have circumvent
Now the decision makers stay and
the Rank & File are stuck
I and my co-workers tried to speak with
them and they passed the buck
Later that day I tried to gather the troops
Let's pull ourselves up by our own boots
But too many of them were in despair
They only focused on what wasn't fair
I wanted to start an investment group
With our own retirement plan to boot
But they didn't want to play the part
They only wanted to return to start
I watched as they prepared for the next task
Of course I knew what they were doing, no need to ask
They are putting themselves back
in the situation of negative
Different workplace where the
attitude is counterproductive
As I stop to think the situation is very sad
Looking to the future it is clear the same
employees will once again be mad

Reading your Sign

You are truly a blessing
What is needed is a history lesson
Emotionally the connection is there
Otherwise there wouldn't be a scare
Release from the emotional steel bars is needed
Your warning has been seriously heeded
No need to fight, no need to fuss
Nothing that can't be worked between us
Events in life may make us stronger
Finding the purpose may take longer
It's all about people in the end
Forget about your so called friend
The devil will lead you on and say it's OK
While behind him your friends are in decay
Watch the warning signs whether you like them or not
Because they are placed firmly on top of the clock
Ready or not time ticks on despite your motivation
If I were you I would watch the hesitation
Blessings are there for a reason
More than likely this very season
If you don't read you might as well go blind
Don't let this day pass, without reading your sign

Road to Success

There's no better road to success than knowing the secret
Others may doubt it a gambler may bet
If you follow the rule you will see a sudden change
Just keep the love for helping others in range

The work place

Do as you are told and you shall not fold.
Follow the template if you are so bold
Go to school learn all you can
At your company you will be top (wo)man
What happens when you get to the top
There may be a chance your income will stop.
But if we work hard it will be fine
Just continue to tow the company line
Executives say the company isn't doing well
They watched last night as the stocks fell
The jobs are suddenly cut
The process seems so abrupt
Just last month they patted us on the back
Now our entire department is under attack
Some of their decisions didn't seem quite right
Those extra investments weren't very bright
Now life goes as unemployment begins to sore
Meanwhile those who did wrong make millions more
Of course the unemployed must insist
They put themselves on someone's call list
Although it may appear insane
We must find employment and do it again
It doesn't take long to figure it out
The rank and file doesn't have much clout
Rationally you must insist
The entrepreneur takes all the risk
But there is some risk as well at the bottom of the pole
As all of this moving around begins to take its toll
There is a family who is affected by
others who don't know the name
Humans begin to feel we are part of
some big corporate game
It is no place to shed your personal life
At the same time it can get you out of your strife
You may know a lot but remain in the same position

But the boss's buddy may present the
award winning acquisition
If there is a way out maybe it's better to take it
Many individual ideas may be the perfect fit
Without them the corporate agenda wouldn't exist today
Take a moment we want to hear what you have to say
Leave the rat race alone for the moment, it will be OK.
The company will survive rather you get the job or not
Think of this when away from loved
ones watching the clock
You ask for the job then complain day and night
Think for a moment and see why this may not be right
When the settlers left England it wasn't to work for others
It was to find a better life for our sisters and brothers
But while you are there make the workplace work for you
As you are there put yourself in a different shoe
It won't take long for you to figure out
You are one of the people with a lot of clout

Weather the storm

Independent thinkers come with innovative ideas
Many have very lucrative careers
Watch what others do and do the opposite
Be persistent and do not quit
Great presidents, inventors and owners join the list
Often they have naysayers in their midst
You may recognize them as cattle
Those who run away from the battle
But the buffalo makes the challenge his home
He has nerves that feel like a stone
As he runs toward the situation where others may flee
The independent thinking says "I" while others say "we"
He is smart and helps others to achieve
His impression on life he will surely leave
Keep in mind there is more than the outer shell
What makes you different also makes you special

SPEAKING
OF
POLITICS

$American Taxpayer$

What I need to do is lay down the facts
You need me to raise your tax
Yet with every increase you appear surprised
However the voting booth is before your very eyes
You need my programs to keep your family in tact
You need my schools so your brain doesn't get lax
Protecting you was the agreement from the start
Understand that military spending is off the chart
You don't need guns to protect your own home
All you need to do is pick up the phone
We will be there with our own gun in hand
We have protection for you throughout the land
But if we find out you were somehow protecting yourself
We may have another arrest under our belt
In some cases your situation my be dire
You may find your home on fire
You need us to come and save your property
That's another reason for the tax, surely you see
Without me, as a citizen you will be at a loss
That is why I must insist that I be your boss
Of course you will groan, moan, and whine
Then come Election Day you will be just fine
Everybody knows the only change is the name
Once we arrive in Washington it's all just the same
Programs you don't need will go up
and our numbers down
But at the end of the day the American tax payer
is the real clown

Anti-American

The constitution gets in my way
It is not relevant what it has to say
Meanwhile, I will alter the meaning to assist me
As I move forward with my agenda you can't see

Attacking the Rich

After all of this time you still have not learned
Every time you come after me you get burned
You want to take what I have earned because you hate
You come up with all of these ideas to retaliate
You say I have more wealth than I can bear
Tax the rich, because it isn't fair
Then you get the politicians to agree
They sit around and come up with some ridiculous fee
It's of course in an effort to come after me
You would think by now you would just relax
At the end of the day you actually pay the tax
You are foolish but it is ok
Perhaps your parents raised you that way
If you would only use that energy to join the ranks
Things aren't as bad as you might think
They say its lonely at the top and there is a reason why
It's because you waste time trying to get me to fry
If there is a tax hike I will prevail
A punishment for my company YOU will fail.
I can only help you if you let me win
Staying where you are is the real sin
Take it from me for I am extremely smart
Take your knowledge and master your art
There is no reason it has to be this way
Perhaps you will figure it out one day.

Illegal Immigration

It took a lot of work to get here and I want to stay
I don't really care what you Americans have to say
As a matter of fact I don't speak your language
It would be better for me if you would change it
The law has been broken go ahead and let it slide
Just realize my home country is where I hold my real pride
The funny part is if I hold a protest to say I am right
You Americans allow me to do it without a fight
Your TV camera is there and my face is everywhere
But I show up and figuratively spit in
your face without a care
Press one for English often is a bother for me to hear
Just make the whole thing my language
is the direction to steer
If you come to my country we are not such a gracious host
This is the part of the argument that amuses me the most
If you come to my country for your
language holds little affection
Don't even think about running for any sort of election
If you are not born there just stay at home
This is the place where MY people roam
Until we decide to take over America
then the rules will change
We expect the royal treatment and all of the gain
You blame corporation for being nice to me
Speaking my language as they greet me with glee
It is my money they want for they are doing what they do
You would understand if you would try on their shoe
No, it is the Government who has failed you yet again
The politicians walk all over you and call me friend
Get over yourself I am here to stay
Kick me out, I will only return another day

Loss of Sight

When I take a walk down the street I may use a stick
Others in ear shot will hear click, click, click
My Seeing Eye dog will often lead the way
He is very faithful I must say
I may listen to the radio and get the news of the day
They are overtaking America overseas, the dollar in decay
On the other side of the globe they want to attack
Yet internally we give one another flack
Raise taxes one politician shouts
It will boost the economy I have no doubt
Go away citizen, no money no clout
Vote for me, I will help you out
Recycle your cans or the earth will fry
Be responsible or she will die
Yet I wonder if the focus is right
Because the terrorist want to kill us tonight
All these challenges in the world you find.
And you have the nerve to call me blind.

Politics as usual

The attack will come from the unguarded threat
An evil dictator whose friendship we will regret
Weapons were tested then denied
Our U.N sanctions were often defied
Now that we are under attack
The share of blame we do not lack
Reactive solutions are underway
Now that we have seen that avoidable day
The situation now looks dismal
Too late to blame the elected official
Many of the people are long gone
But left their helpful policies to carry on

Money 4 me

I will tell you what to do
I will control your life through and through
The goal is to make the currency in your account few
The money is better spent in my hands
It's hard to understand why I don't have many fans
At the end of the day, I really don't care
There is no intent to make my collections fair
Excuses will be made to why I need the funds
Admittedly, some of you stick to your guns
You are so smart and you certainly have a clue
Whatever, the case your tax is now due
Everyday you pay me what I want
I want all of it to be quite blunt
If you go to class I will tax the school
I will encourage teachers to educate fools
They will teach you to rely on me
Do it my way and you will never be free
This system of ours is in my favor
Your hard-earned money I will forever savor
The less you have, the more I will take
So far my income will fill all of the Great Lakes
But what I have won't be discussed
Hand over your earnings without a fuss
I must go and complete my task
Who am I? You may ask
My name is known throughout the land
But feel free to call me, The Taxman

The Assassination of a Leader

The President is now dead
Took a bullet to the head
Although he is gone
His policies will live on
Yet history will likely recall
How on this day he took a fall
History is known to come again
As once again we lose a friend
Some remember a shot at the station
As he remained a ruler of our nation
Others have a theater in mind
The final act he left us behind
In both cases a second term was to come
The shooter knew it, the no good scum
The final shot our leader ruled on
Unlike some predecessors who were six to one
Who knows if he were able to carry on
If only we could have gotten a hold of that gun
So far each has paid in their own way
But it doesn't change the outcome I must say
We voted him in lets keep him in tact
Let the next election be the final act

The Cheating Game

We know you cheated on your wife
She gave you so much of her life
You look surprised as she crushes things
Amazed at the grief your action brings
If you are a public figure we see it everyday
In some cases the person at the mic may be gay
But when it's public the wife is often by his side
Saying how her spouse is loving and she will let it slide
Because in the politicians case he
may be up for re-election
We must deny the charges and
explain, there was no erection
No thanks to the visits to the hotel rooms
your marriage is on display
Amazingly in almost every case the
husband has one thing to say
I didn't think I would get caught nor my
marriage go south in decay
Or my wife was being a pain in the butt anyway
But the male spectator is often confused
by the cheaters choice
As he watches the news you can hear
the confused man's voice
Why did he sleep with her when his wife is such a looker?!?
Yet, the woman he chose looks like such a hooker
Depending on your political party will
determine if you should run again
If you are the right politician it could gain you some friends
Yet at the end of the day it doesn't matter which game
Your marriage to your beloved will never be the same.

The Terrorist

I came in and slowly took away your rights
What's funny is more was given to me without a fight
I killed your American servicemen
trying to protect your freedom
Then you turn around and give me the rights
I took from him
Your country is amazing how some citizens
protest to protect me
Then I snuff out the life of your people
with happiness and glee
Your focus was on the servicemen
issuing blindfolds and having sex
Instead of on me withholding information
on the next arms test
Even when I admit I killed thousands of your people
You protect me as you would a church steeple
In the meantime I live on and the rest of you debate
While my brothers hide out in caves and discuss your fate
The only thing slowing us down now
is the military in our face
But it won't be long before you put another
sympathetic politician in place
One that will stop the military from killing all of us
Then we will come to your land and kill without a fuss
The little attention spent monitoring your borders is a joke
The time spent wondering why I hate you
says there is no hope
But it goes deeper than that I am happy to report
Your citizens are prisoners in their own airport
But I am patient and do little work on my own
Your people won't even listen to me on the telephone
Yet if I want to know which terrorist has lit the latest fuse
All I have to do is turn on the news
Your media has no loyalty to its own land
The excuses by journalist are just plain bland

They refuse to understand that our loyalty is to a few
If I had the chance I would kill them too
They don't even have the decency to call me a terrorist
I guess we will just have to wait until the very next blast

The Tracking of Spychips

When it is explained in the beginning it all sounds good.
We are told great things are coming to our neighborhood.
If an item is stolen you can tell the merchant where
Or track an abducted child whose parents
had quite a scare
If a suspect is committing a crime
Police will be there right on time.
But time went by and other things began to take place
You began to use technology to alter the human race
My identity is no longer mine but belongs to corporate
You know where I bank, shop and the size of my zit
This information is mine not yours I say
We are here to help you, it will be OK
But since this new technology I only see demise
Meanwhile my insurance rates are on the rise
You don't like what I eat or where I drive
According to you my credibility is less than five
You punish me through the sins of others
I watch helplessly as you monitor my brothers
Meanwhile electronic eyes consistently view us all
We imagine Big Brother must be having a ball
Slowly we allowed them to take away our rights
One bill at a time without putting up much of a fight
Even worse they returned to office time and again
Each campaign they called us their friend
Now today as we finally stop and take a look
We learn that "1984" wasn't just a book

United Nations

Let's all come together and strive as one
Together we will make the world more fun
We will protect our world from the bad guy
With our unified brain power we can reach the sky
The evil dictator will make threat of an attack
Like disciplining a spoiled child we say. Don't do that!
We will issue a sanction which will make you stop
Of course down the road the resolution will be a flop
You will continue to build your weapons
and thumb your nose
This will continue until your project has come to a close
Then we will insist on other alternative solution
While you continue your rage of execution
One or two on the council may disagree
but it won't matter
During the summit there may be similar chatter
We will continue to be the do nothing
group with a sense of purpose
While the rest of the world doesn't appear to notice us
This is good because there is corruption in our own ranks
We have the International media to give thanks
If there happens to be a war there will be no blue helmets
We will only send soldiers over to baby sit
the ladies and gents
Firing a shot may cause someone to get hurt
This debate of course is older than dirt
But if you disagree we will say you have no compassion
Never mind the dictator who will kill his own son
We don't understand freedom and what it is like to lose it
If we did we would try to keep the nation fit
Out with the dictator who wants to rule the world
Often for the gain of diamonds and pearls
Sometimes it's for the pure idea of control
With the U.N they will find a huge hole
To move ahead in their single minded theory

To make the world more dark and dreary.
Speak up and join the voice of the International People
But if you disagree, you will be marked
as weak and feeble
Meanwhile our policies will cut you like a knife
Enjoy it now, before we allow the dictator
to destroy your life

We are Family

I see you are low on cash
Trust me and with your creditors you won't clash
The money will come from me for I am here for you
I am always here if you don't know what to do
If you are having challenges raising your young
In one of my fine establishments is where they belong
After all the rich is the reason you are where you are
But stick with me and you will go far
Your employer has done you wrong
With my programs you won't be poor for long
Depend on me and together we will climb
Your life will only improve just trust your mind
Do you recall all I have done?
Lots of subsidies for everyone
All we have to do is go to the treasury
Just let the well to do pay for the fee
If it weren't for us you would have no money
The rich is stealing from you, they think it's funny
No need to thank me I have your best interest at heart
Let's raise taxes again, that would be a good start
Just remember when it's time
What to do to make things fine
I will show you much affection
If you remember me during the election
That's right, remember who I am
Just cast a vote for your Uncle Sam

Government's Role

The truth should unfold
That is the government's role
Protect the citizens from unrest
Put our enemies to the test
The dictator will not be appeased
He will bring our country to its knees
The military will prevail
Their form of leadership will fail
The programs often lose sight
It may get in the way of the fight
Without freedom it doesn't matter
If with the constitution we shatter
Somehow the government lost the fact
As we fail to keep the constitution in tact
The focus appears to be on raising the tax
Less focus on the actual required act
Rules and regulations can keep us tame
Sometimes political gain is used for fame
The role of the government must remain clear
Misuse of government won't keep us here

Pre will set us free

The sky is the limit let's take advantage
We have a new country and they want vengeance.
What we will do is outline freedom
We won't let rulers bind us again
Untied we will stand
Justice must prevail
Put the bad guys in jail
The government will provide defense
Of course this is common sense
Love is great but we need freedom
We must be prepared when they come
As we fight to protect our Liberty
Insure our domestic tranquility
This will pave the way for prosperity
The pursuit is done because we are free
If we stick to our principles they will be jealous
They are sure to come for us
Future generations will understand
Together we will lend a helping hand
It doesn't matter as we build our nest
Because we have the right to pursue happiness

Road to Success

There is no better road to success than knowing the secret
Others may doubt it a gambler may bet
If you follow the rule, you will see a sudden change
Just keep the love for helping others in range
If you represent others, keep your morals in tact
Do what you can to keep the nation in the black
Plato actually had the process under attack
If you are too smart to engage then later, you may be burned
You are punished by those who failed to learn
If you take the road to success, others may follow
Your personality should not be shallow
C students teach A students but you must prevail
The road to success is something they will never tell
If the corporation wants to hold you back
Come up with your own plan of attack
Before you reach the end of the road, others will be bold
First, you must get past you
Then the exterior may keep you blue
If you get around the corporations, you are doing well
Now the government will encourage you to fail
Just remember if the road is bumpy its probably correct
Keeping the journey consistent your life is set
The road to success can be bumpy and winding
Just think of the joy this journey may bring
You may take the well-paved street
Thinking you have life beat
If you don't want what they have
then let them keep the bait
Otherwise, it is clear to everyone exactly your fate
Take the other road less traveled
then tell others your discovery
They will follow only if they want to be free

Democracy

You say you are the servant
Later you imply this isn't what you meant
Many promises were made during the campaign
As they are carried out it doesn't seem the same
During the research it is learned of the contributions
Because of this there are now retributions
The classes are now concerned about our vote
We realize now we are in the same boat
The classes that were adversaries during the election
Now find ourselves trying to make
the necessary correction
We live in a great democracy
Where voter and candidate pay a fee
Before either candidate will quit
They must prove the other unfit
The part that causes such a fright
Is that both parties are right
You may doubt in how you select
The system is not perfect
There is the part the founding fathers documented
Then there are the sections that were circumvented
It doesn't matter where you stand
This land is our land
Stand tall and don't let democracy fail
Through it all as people we will prevail
Together we can do what's fit
People broke it, people can fix it

Your Reflection

If you want a glimpse at your self image look around
Your friends and associates will bound
Your spouse will enlighten
Your day will be brightened
Take this small premise and move it out
Find out what your county is all about
Complaints to the politicians are directed
You say your beliefs aren't being protected
Your representatives don't represent at all
Claiming your integrity is taking a fall
Take a look in the mirror and find out the cause
You may quickly discover quite a number of flaws
No one is perfect, not even the person whom you voted
Your request for a better country are duly noted
But there are lobbyist who have an even lower self image
Who put their self interest out front with a vengeance
If you are looking for a weak link, watch the self esteem
The lowest one still attempts to rise with the cream
Identify these individuals before they get out front
Or your nation will receive the brunt
Sometimes if you go with the tide you may drown
You may be forced to watch others go down
Look at yourself and make the necessary adjustment
Then watch as others benefit from what is sent
It will be returned to you as you serve your community
Your efforts your neighbors will clearly see
Your community will improve
Your no good politicians will move
The nation will continue to be a reflection
The difference is a more improved nation

SPEAKING OF LIFE AND DEATH

Death

Many blame me for things they don't understand
Actually life and I go hand in hand
We are brothers and see one another daily
But he is the favorite as others defy me
The truth of the matter is I don't know more than you
I am given a schedule and with that you turn blue
There is a transition that must take place
This is all I do to keep with the pace
People call my brother short which is just fine
He is offering you an opportunity,
he doesn't know the time
Sometimes if I have warning I will give him a hint
Then the show is over you have performed your stint
I take you from this life into another
It all depends on the time spent with my brother
Because your soul comes with me
and your body left behind
It all depends on how well you read your sign
How you are remembered will be your best indicator
That's the best I can do, I'm not a dictator
Only the messenger with a message for you today
My brother wants to prepare you for your stay
Of course he can be hard at times but that's OK
He only wants to prepare you for my arrival
If you don't believe me just read your bible
Because he may bend the rules even if you become sicker
Unfortunately my orders are a bit stricter
Your soul can only leave the shell
It's not often I am allowed to reschedule
But take my advice now before it is too late
You never know when you will learn your fate.

Family Affair

Raising a child must be ok
I will get pregnant and see what society has to say
The child will be good looking better than all the rest
When you compare my baby pictures my child looks best
But there are some things to consider as life goes by
Such as getting out of bed when you hear the baby cry
The child is dependant and can't live with out me
Whenever we go out somebody will be paid a fee
At this point I should go and leave
the child for someone else to raise
It's as though this time period will go on
and the child won't leave this phase
The crying the unhappy camper because
he needs to be changed
My entire life overnight has been completely rearranged
When they are little they are so sweet, cuddly and cute
But at 16 they change, wanting the car keys,
the whole things a hoot
Next thing you know they are off to college
Previously thinking they are superior in knowledge
Then reality sets in and you talk to your child on the phone
It is apparent that he is not coming home
The love I had for you and all that I did bear
That day I didn't know where you were,
it was quite a scare
Now your life moves on and it doesn't include me
What I wouldn't give now to pay that additional fee
But it's a one way ticket in life
with no opportunity for return
Looking at our family portrait it's that bright day I yearn
But family values is where it starts
to make you a great adult
Your love for me will live on and will always be felt

Before there was student affairs,
minority affairs and all the other stuff
Let's keep it in perspective and disregard the fluff
Without a strong foundation your life will be in despair
It all comes back to the family affair

Family Planning

I want to pick the look of my child
It is my right to choose a certain smile
Hollywood is expecting a certain look
He will be a big star if I go by the book
On second thought, why bother
They tell me I can pick a daughter
With hair beyond her shoulder
She will be beautiful, even when she's older
Blue hair blonde eyes
Brown hair may take the prize
As a parent the power is in my hands
It is obvious, where I stand

Early Out

If others have let you down there is still hope
Sometimes life is difficult to cope
Getting out ahead of time will not end well
It is better if you live to tell
Be sure to make an appointment
Someone will give you a hint
Life is short
Yet some abort
If you are able to hack
You may actually come back
But usually it's one way
Making it your last day
Taking the chance
You shorten your dance
It's a crime
Although they missed the signs
When you are in despair
Someone does care
Maybe they didn't appear real
Perhaps they have their own burden to deal
Just tell them your plan
Chances are, they will understand

Finding your Why

Moving forward with the answer will make it easier
Otherwise in death your life may be a blur
Finding the reason to make it right
Discovering the answer to take a bite
Your dreams should soar higher than a kike
Higher than a rocket in full throttle flight
Stop and think because it won't appear by magic
Only you can come up with that perfect fit
It is a dream all your own, that no one can steal
Through your day to day actions you can make it real
Use this tool to raise your commitment level
Use your wisdom to avoid the devil
He will come in disguise to steal your dream
The situation may not be as it may seem
Stay strong and keep your course
When you get old, have no remorse
Commitment, dedication and knowing what you want
If you must, write it in a different font
Keep it in front of you so you don't forget
Don't live your life as one big regret
Keep it in front of you to keep your path clear
Maybe it's for family, travel or out of fear
Make up your mind, you just can't stay here
Everyday try and keep your cool
Be sure to make your "Why" your escape jewel
Carve it, shape it, make it shine
Your why will get you out of this bind
Of course your strength comes from above
It's what dreams are made of

Giving you a line

The line is smaller than the number
Yet, this is what people will remember
How you use the line today
Will influence when you don't see another day
The numbers only tell the beginning and end
Think of the people who call you friend
The road less traveled is the one you should be on
Think of the many lives you have won
These people will explain your line
Express to others your life was just fine
People remember you by who you are
No matter how near or far
Learn to serve others and their lives will be touched
It will explain why your life means so much

Hour Glass

Your occupation keeps you occupied
You help keep the economy supplied
Is it what you do or who you are?
People get this confused by far
When you meet someone new
The initial questions are few
You ask what you do.
This somehow defines
Keeping you blind
Unable to find
Stop and think!
What about the person on the inside
What is it the position may hide?
That may camouflage the pride
The true nature of one
That life has shun
Know the way
Before decay
Start today
O.K?

If

Perhaps, maybe, might or should have
Often words of regret as you look back
Proverbs says man without vision shall perish
Those words are not used because he says shall
Which means it is going to happen
Live your own life, don't let others live it for you
Often in life people are happy to tell you what to do
Your employer, the government, your spouse
Taking a walk down this path you will find lots of company
Once you arrive at the end of this journey
many others will await you
All too often your fellow sheep will have one commonality
The use of maybe, might or should've.
We are bound to make mistakes because
this is what makes us human
What we do with these mistakes is what makes
us stronger or weaker
If you ask any of our great leaders past
or present the answer is common
Many will admit mistakes were made along
the way yet they moved forward
True to form only quitters quit and winners win
You can't keep a quitter from quitting and
you can't keep a winner down
Being blessed to make it to an old age
is just that-a blessing
The same as being brought in the world
was a great gift from beyond
Once in your elderly stage there are bound to be
regrets big and small
Be sure to regret the things you did, verses
the opportunities that got away.

If tomorrow never comes

Procrastination is key to failure
This only works if you concur
The road to success has many road blocks
Internal and external forces keep you in a box
Wait until tomorrow and do it then
It's relaxing to call procrastination friend
Cases may occur where this is fine
But time may protest putting you in a bind
Time may expire and your goal cut short
Forcing your plans to result in abort
Tomorrow arrives and you are not around
Your presence no where to be found
Steps could have been taken to make it right
Your future of loved ones could have been bright
No need to ponder what could have been
Today is the time you will score a win
Tomorrow is not promised and yesterday is gone
Do something in the present and your name carries on
Wait until tomorrow and the opportunity is gone
If tomorrow never comes it will be a great loss
Take the initiative and make success your boss
There will be a time when you will face the expiration
Now is the time to avoid hesitation
Plan for tomorrow but work for today
This may be the only time you will have your say.

Judgment by the King

Your trial is near have you prepared your defense
One is not needed even if you are on the fence
You were told this day would come
The King will judge your fate before it's all done
If you know him you may pass it all together
Being friends with the King will make it much better
In fact if he says he doesn't know you your chance is gone
He will sentence you to the place where you belong
You can't say you weren't told
That argument is very old
He will listen to what you have to say
Then he will cast you away
The trial date is set and we will all be there
Only those who have done wrong will say it isn't fair
The necessary corrections must be made ahead of time
Or you will find yourself in a very serious bind
Discover what is important before your trial date
Otherwise you may not enjoy your required fate
Get to know your King while he is on your side
Your biggest downfall may actually be your pride
It's much better to listen to what he has to say
This way what you have in store is a brighter day
You will live forever if you do it right
Your future with him will be extremely bright

LIFE

If only I could find the meaning you say
It's better if you got on your knees and pray
I'm in you, around you and a part of you
But it is too late once you are blue
Many will find me later after I leave
While others stay behind and grieve
You stay too busy often not giving me a second look
You won't find the definition resting in a self help book
There is a place you will find me
You will learn one way or the other you see
Your creator knows the answer
and wishes to save your soul
Yet you treat me worst than your soon to be hole
I am happening now, was happening then,
and forever more
Yet you are busy consumed with an unfulfilling chore
You can't keep me lying about collecting dust on the shelf
Because I continue while you are off doing something else
The greatest value that will ever be
You can't purchase or trade you see
It's a one time deal where if you are smart
you will do what you feel
Because the offer I make to you couldn't be more real
Because he is coming, His arrival is guaranteed
The smartest decision you could ever make
is to believe in me
When he gets here I can no longer help
His presence upon you will be truly felt.
But if you have listened and valued me like you should
Then our goals will be for the common good
That it is great news we will boast
Because eternally we will meet our main host

Live to Tell

Your story should be told long after you are gone
The life you lived was short yet your legend long
Before the story is turned to set a political agenda
I must tell others what you meant to her
Once you are gone others may get it wrong
Although you left your name to carry on
So much is at our disposal where it should be right
Unlike our forefathers where we lost the reason
for their fight
We get it wrong on purpose to fit the political template
The school system does not want to teach
something they will regret
Textbooks are written in an effort not to offend
The truth about what happened
administrators will quickly bend
The lie isn't blatant but from a slanted perspective
Keep the truth alive beyond the life you live
Keep it going so the children of tomorrow do not forget
If you take the knowledge to your grave,
you may just regret
You do not know what you don't know
Too often young minds will go with the flow.
It may only be later that what is learned
isn't exactly how it was
The story retold simply because it creates the proper buzz
Since the beginning of time the story has been told
Disbelievers want to leave the information out in the cold
Live to tell the historical secret that you know so well
Be sure not to fall under the political spell
Pass the information to those who will listen
Do your part and the information will glisten
If your Grandparents or great grandparents want to speak
Be sure they understand that it is their knowledge you seek
You must carry on once they are gone
It is up to you to help them carry on

If you are fortunate, you will help the information to fit
After all, those who don't remember the past
are condemned to repeat it

Man vs. Gerbil

The gerbil runs on his wheel
To him he has a sweet deal
He runs around and around
The gerbil eats food from the ground
It appears he thinks he is going somewhere
The wheel impedes, it isn't fair
Man may look at the gerbil and laugh
With colors he has mapped out his own graph
It's time for work, the spectator must go
His performance begins soon, time for the show
Yes boss, no boss, my team made a mistake
How many more years can a person take
Work is over, the day now ends
Tomorrow we will do it again
Tomorrow we will make the stockholders proud
In the process, it will put my career on a cloud
Away he goes trying to cut another deal
Incidentally, what is the difference between
man and the Gerbil's wheel?

Missing your Exit

You are on the Highway to nowhere moving very fast
Completely unaware that your lifestyle can not last
It appears you are at top speed
as you race with such a rage
Not taking a moment to pause and look at your gauge
If you took the time maybe you would stop for a bit
More immediately you would get off at the next exit
Because at some point the highway will continue
and you will not
Some of your friends and family
will experience a big shock
Because as you pass others on the way to your destination
No mere mortal can deny the basis of his/her creation
Roads bridges and highways can be built all day long
Reading your sign to the proper exit won't steer you wrong
At some point and time your tank will run dry
Your exit will be long behind you
and you may wonder why
There can't be anything wrong
because my song is still alive
This maybe true, yet there are other positions
besides just drive
Improper maintenance of your transportation
mode can't be fixed
At the end of your personal journey you
may find you missed your exit

Misunderstanding

They say that seeing is believing
With you there is no deceiving
Maybe we can get together for lunch
An awesome conversation is my hunch
It's easy how the fun did flow
Maybe we can do a show
But it just wasn't right
You didn't show up that night
They say that seeing is believing
Being together is achieving
I rang your phone there was no answer
Your roommate said check the banister
It's strange there was no fight
Yet you didn't show up that night
We seem to connect on a lot
This relationship certainly has a shot
Your fears should be put to rest
Our connection has been put to the test
You can run but you can't hide
It is in yourself you must confide
The information is already out
Others can hear your heart shout
But earlier it whispered to me
With you her emotions are free
But with it comes promise, hope & fear
It is advised that this be held dear
Soon you will embark on a battle
Then your heart will quickly rattle
Tell her what you think
Then things will go down the sink
If you run hide & don't care
Then your love you will share
If there truly is a misunderstanding
It will be a rough emotional landing
If seeing is believing

Then you were just leaving
Think of all that has been said
The words swimming in our heads
But the clarification should be clear
Because together we have nothing to fear
The misunderstanding we must dismiss
Believe me, both our hearts will insist

Moving on

If you knew the date
What difference would this make?
How would you alter what you do?
Would you make your sins few?
Or would you go the other extreme?
Perhaps be clearly mean
Your creditors may be in disarray
What would they have to say?
It's possible a loan they would not lend
Their policy they will not bend
Your religious affairs are another matter
Would you actually focus away from the latter?
How would you use the time to utilize your soul?
Or would you not care, to be so bold?
Under this scenario the 10 Commandment exist
You still don't know the day after is the gist
The point is you are now gone
Your name is left to carry on
What is increased is knowledge of your appointment
Others may decide what your life meant
Some may know under a gloomy circumstance
Others it will occur by happenstance
You will still have the opportunity to work non-stop
Take your career to the very top
You may also spend time with your family
Which option do you foresee?
If not knowing would change your choice
Why does the unknown have such a loud voice?
At this point we can only speculate
Keeping in mind you actually do know your fate

Music

My fans want to hold me close
I can change their mood they often boast
The ability to fill a coliseum is mine
The low key say filing their room is fine
My creator has a special gift
The opportunity to give your spirit a lift
It's interesting some of them couldn't hear
Others blindly produced without fear
The flow appears seamless
My influence on society is endless
Many different genres make it appear seamless
Different generations and the same notes
Some of my compositions may give you hope
Fame has been offered to those who don't deserve
While others now have the opportunity to serve
Fortune and fame has taken them to the spotlight
Where they can make the wrongs into the right
Others just want to appreciate
Being thankful they have what it takes
To have the full enjoyment where you can time travel
Or use descriptions on how your life is to unravel
Whatever you want I can help you move on
I am music and I can do it in just one song

Not Guilty

Innocence is your middle name you say.
Persuasion is used to push your critics away
Everyone is picking on you with accusations
In the midst of it all you fail to gain a revelation
Accusing you of things you say you haven't done
Stating you didn't pull the trigger on the gun
Or saying you are a good person overall
Stating it's the other person who has the gall
They did it you were only standing by
Maybe you should speak up, don't be shy
Association is the part way to success
Be a good influence to others is my guess
If you continue to run with a bad crowd
Your quiet voice won't be heard if they are loud
Some of your best people have gotten lost in the shuffle
All because there are some feathers you refuse to ruffle
Meanwhile your name is taken through the mud
This type of cleansing can't be solved by the tub
Just remember how we arrived at that name
It remains unclear why the doctor played the game
The point is made at the end of the day
Your behavior will reflect what others say
You may think it is all in fun
However, you can't run with the skunks
and not smell like one

One Day Early

It is clear that your time will come one day
Its better if you live to be old and grey
We don't know precisely when that time will come
It's certainly a situation you can't out run
However, in certain situations you may slow it down
Longevity will assist you if you keep your feet on the ground
The importance of this may not appear relevant
Your assistance on this earth may be heaven sent
Your influence may make all of the difference
Take a moment and take a look at the inference
Tomorrow you were to die but you lived your life wrong
You lived your life with destruction and
today you can't be strong
You grow weaker and weaker and you are to lose one day
All due to your negligence you can't
tell us what you have to say
Tomorrow you were to conceive a life
with great wisdom and ability
Someone with a cure that would save many constantly
Think of the poor farmer who helped
others when he didn't try
That faithful day in Scotland where in
the distance he heard a cry
A boy fell into the Fenchi but without
hesitation the boy he would save
Two days later an upstanding citizen came
calling saying the farmer was brave
The man in the very elegant form of
transportation was grateful for the act
He realized what had happened the
day before and laid out the facts
The well to do gentleman offered to
repay the farmer for saving his son
He stood near his boy grateful for the
life that was previously won

The offer that was made to the farmer
was of gratitude and profit
The Farmer being a good man did not
accept for he did not want return
The well to do stranger offered the
farmers' son a way to learn
It is this offer the Good Samaritan could not refuse
A good education is something his son could use
The benefit for others soon followed through
As the lad invented medicine that could help you
However the story doesn't stop there as
the third Reich gained control
One other stranger of this tale would be so bold
To stand up against Hitler in his reign of nothing but bad will
If he would have been lost that day there
would have been no Winston Churchill
Positioning this story can been seen in many ways
The images of these men can be found in many plays
There is nothing to act out if the players are gone
Better to stay a day late, and have your name carry on

Perception

Your world view varies from where you stand
Many say they are happy in this great land
A cynic will have a certain viewpoint
which is often negative
Where as an optimist will be completely
happy with how he lives.
Think about the disagreements that
take place on any given day
They often are derived from what someone else has to say
One person can deliver the same speech
and have it reach the same place
Yet some will love it while others say the
speechgiver is in poor taste
Surverying social psychology of things
help to make this world bizarre
Analyzing the methods of expermintation
may take the limits of man too far
The electroschock therapy was certainly false in the end
But with the Milgrim experiments man didn't quite win
It keeps the marketing people on their toes
As they struggle to find the right shows
Something that will generate money for the client
They hope the profit they make will feed a giant

Posting Bond

Spend, spend, spend let the money roll out
Wall Street loves us there is no doubt
Look at the bull as he dances with praise
Out of our profits we offer exec a 49% raise
Now the bear has arrived and he is not our friend
It's interesting how our shareholders
aren't with us to the end
Everyone wishes to bail after all we have done
Historically it's clear the Rank & File didn't have fun
Some of them warned us the future may be bleak
But our heads were inflated and our souls very weak
But as always we have a solution which has a lot of clout
We will just have the government bail us out
After all if they don't save us our land will go a stray
Do this quickly while we keep the media at bay
Meanwhile we will post blame and give the CEO the boot
He shouldn't worry because he is being
supplied a Golden Parachute
The whole ordeal makes me chuckle
because the whole time it was OK
Probably the biggest problem was spending your 401k
Ironically you will need the money to
give to your representative
Right now exactly how much we will get is a bit tentative
But no need to worry about us, I know
this idea you are not fond
The government will raise your taxes
in an effort to pay our bond

Temp to Perm

Spring Summer Winter & fall
For a season, you can have it all
Tell me your desire; I will be your friend
I will wait for you once the season ends
Money, fortune or fame
Your wish will be fulfilled again & again
Spring is here, look at the pretty colors
You will enjoy life, like no other
Guess what? Here's a tip
This summer you should take a trip
Winter is here don't forget your skis
Go to the lodge & do what you please
Enjoy life from top to bottom
I will be with you this autumn
Now that the season has ended its time to go
Take my hand as we travel below
While you were asleep, I was awake
Plotting on logistics on your soul to take
As anticipated, the season is gone
You will find this next phase quite long
It's interesting you say I'm not fair
That this place is too much for you to bear
It was clear from the beginning there are no buts
To put it in perspective, I hate your guts
The appearances were before your very eyes
Nothing but beauty as I appeared in disguise.
You failed to remember the reason for the season
The opportunity as they saw the sunrise
Too bad for me I won't get the prize
Soon you will find out what the seasons meant
As you find your next step will be quite permanent

The Music Lives On

The words you sang rang true
Plus no one could sing the Star Spangled Banner Like you
A father should watch out for a child and treat him right
Instead he put a bullet in you in the middle of the night
Four years prior a stranger took on this role
Yet he created the same sort of hole
This man with one of the greatest
bands sang of a revolution
With him it was clear to see mans day by day evolution
I often wondered what it would have been to see all four
As we sit around and watch all of
the screaming fans adore
Let's stop these people from robbing
us of such great talent
Meanwhile as they walk the earth
don't take them for granted
True that people of great power abuse
it with their own problems
Hollywood and the media do very little to help solve them
The clock tics on and it's another day without you
The spectators would have done the
same if life was on the other shoe
They are gone and they aren't coming back
Many after them find it's their talent they lack
For right now let's remember the music and the joy
People who caught the eye and ear of one little boy

The Seven Headed Monster

The seven headed monster will grow all heads
That will be the beginning of the end, enough said

Time Travel

If you break the time barrier, you have
traveled the speed of light
The number 186,000 miles per second is always right
It never changes although the observer
may change his perspective
Velocity equals distance traveled no
matter how crazy the objective
If you wish to travel through time, you can
move in the direction of the future
You may return to earth and find the
results to aging holds its own cure
Actually, the transaction you conduct may be quite quick
Just remember time and distance are not fixed
Nevertheless, if you travel through time
the results may appear fine
When you return you may find a burden on your shoulder
Because now all of your friends and family are now older
Let us say you want to go back to the way things were
At this point, it is with Einstein's theory
where reality may occur
You can only travel in one direction
At this point with your loved ones, you may lose affection
To them much time has elapsed
With you only a short period you have grasped
It is relative in the world of time
Moving in that direction may put you in a bind
But is clear that the theory is for real
However putting the numbers into play your life it may steal

Who goes there?

Hyphenated names will divide us
That sort of attitude will pose a fuss
The more you use them the greater the division
The sooner you return home, the better our vision
There is no room for your dispute
Your patriotism we must refute
Please return to where you most desire
Stop living your life here as a liar

SPEAKING OF LOVE

A child's interpretation

A parent says they love their child
In a child's mind this is filed
As the clock tics the mind wonders
Perhaps there was some sort of blunder
Mommy and daddy say they care
But they are always over there
They are often gone it's not fair
When they do this it is a scare
I know how to spell
You should be able to tell
I want you to be with me
I spell time T.I.M.E

Beauty Inside and out

You are so beautiful it's easy to see
When I look at you it makes me feel free
Your legs are so sexy it makes my eyes come out
When other guys look at you we want to start a bout
Your skin so smooth, your eyes so inviting
Seriously, if we were pure animals there would be fighting
But in a way there is a battle among men
Each of us vying to see you again
Your personality so giving and so warm
Yet your body has the perfect form
There are many charities you promote and want to do well
Your actions toward mankind is
leadership, everyone can tell
Your own family can always count on you to be there
No other woman compares to you, it's almost unfair.
You walk through life with such confidence and flair
The most unfortunate part is sometimes
people only see the outside
Other women say they are jealous they often confide
But it is better to have the objective point of view
That is, you are a beautiful person through and through

Boy Meets Girl

The first day of school and I want to stay home
Why can't Mom & Dad just leave me alone?
My mom & I arrive at class
The ride there went very fast
The teacher had me sit next to a girl
For a second I thought I was going to hurl
Once we arrived in elementary school she was my friend
We said we would be friends until the end
One day I was waiting for Jill so that we may play
Then our teacher informs me; Jill has moved away
So sad it is to be alone
Perhaps she is happy in her new home
Now I am in High School and some appear fake
I am not sure how much of this I can take
Then I saw her it had been such a long time
I told her staying away must be a crime
Just then this large young man looked at me with a snarl
She turned to me and said meet my new boyfriend Carl
All through high school the two were an item
Girls would come after me and sometime I would let them
But we were friends just the same
Getting together for double dates
Playing our teenage games
She was with Carl, I was with Jenny
It's funny how our friendship was complimentary
The week before we embarked on higher learning
Something happened that had long been burning
Jill came to me with tears in her eyes
She learned that Carl had taken Jenny as his prize
As I heard from others then Jill confessed
That night at the party she made Carl's face a mess
When she and I arrived at the university
much was laid to rest
We put a lot of concentration on studying for our test

We became closer than ever during those four years
At this moment I can still hear the cheers
It's funny how a person can go through life
Because on this day, I made Jill my wife

Clearing It Up

Don't wish to complicate,
just want to communicate.
You are so sweet and kind,
A love like yours is hard to find.

Commitment

One step at a time in the right direction will get you there.
Even if you only make it by a hair.
You may move ahead at a full sprint
There are questions to where your energy went
Other days you may walk
Some nights you may balk
Let's face it after all
You may be forced to crawl
If you stay the course you may discover
That your commitment is like no other
The goal may be the same
Although it would be foolish to expect fame
Rather you run, walk, stroll or crawl
Stick to your guns and you may have it all
Just remember what your goal may mean
Understand the path to victory is often lean
Know why you do what you do
It's easier to know why success is gained by few
Stick to what's right
Give it all your might
Your commitment may be noticed but not acknowledged
Perhaps because viewers don't posses the knowledge
It doesn't matter just review your list
Your reward is coming and that's the gist

Emotional ties to a woman

It is said a man does not express his feelings
Perhaps during a ballgame he appears the realist
But often the same compassion isn't made
His heart on his sleeve is seldom laid
Perhaps if the male species were to open his heart
This expression of love to his woman would be a great start
Because in many cases his love for her isn't clear
Sometimes the man may tell you this is out of fear
Wondering if his friends would think he is weak
Or perhaps the woman he shows
interest will think he's a freak
But if a man loves a woman it may not hurt to flaunt it
She may even reciprocate if she knows she is wanted
Because there is nothing more dedicated
when she loves you back
You will find her feeling for you will have no slack
Her love for you is real if you would just stick around
Often the male is fooled into thinking
he is perceived as a clown
She will look up to you as head of household
Your decision making concise and bold
But in the time of crises she will help bail you out
Because your love together will win every bout
Your skin so smooth your lips so soft your voice silky smooth
When a man is with you there is no way he can lose.

Jealous Girlfriend

The jealous girlfriend is on the prowl
When woman say hello she yells foul
It is often a case of low esteem
Lucky for me I keep my nose clean

Love

Love is complicated and it can be sweet
During the right moments the world is at your feet
People will do things because they care.
It may not work out, which isn't fair.
It was your parents who introduced you to the world
As they provided life for a boy and a girl
They taught you how to love and care for others
It started with caring for your sisters and brothers
As time went on you wanted to spend quality time
With people you refused to leave behind
If you are lucky enough to find that special someone
That person who remains even when
you are under the gun
Then you are blessed and thank God for that person
Because often in life you may only find one
Love is something you don't understand
You may fall for someone who is rather bland
It only matters what you think and not of another
Remember your parents taught you not to go any further
Now the time has come for you to move on
To teach your children before life has actually begun

Love from afar

You complain that your boyfriend
treats you with no respect
Yet the relationship you are in you don't regret
The very person who will treat you well is told your woes
But those people are treated as the actual foe.
There is someone whom you may call friend
That is the person who will be with you until the end
Good news is that person may often stand by
Offering you a strong shoulder as you continue to cry
The truth of the matter lies at your feet
A successful love life you fail to greet
He arrives late and his excuses are shallow
When it comes to your business he is like a shadow
Wanting to know where you are night and day
His behavior may continue until he is grey
As he walks in you pretend to sleep
Denying to yourself he is such a creep
You look the other way and rollover
He walks through the door and looks you over
You say you love him and refuse to open your eyes
Your lack of emotional freedom will lead to your demise
If you love him like you say you do there
wouldn't be so much heartache
If he loved you like he says he does
your heart he wouldn't break
The days of questions and nights of
confusion you continue to take
Your happiness in this relationship you continue to fake
There is someone who cares for you very much
He would move the earth for you the mountains and such
The chance he would take if only you would give
If only you would choose a different life to live
There is someone who loves you from afar
He may be available by plane or by car

But you will never know which because
you are too occupied
With a love that was gained because someone lied
If it's not too late grab your heart and run
There is plenty of love out there waiting for you to come
Your comfort zone will keep you in your present place
So far you have been moving at the wrong pace
You can do better just let it flow
Just grab your stuff and go

SPEAKING OF MONEY

Debt

The control will take your head under water
While their life will be sucked from your son and daughter
The roof over your head removed and your bed seized
Finance isn't yours to do as you please
If you don't own it, it isn't yours
Meanwhile I can limit the opening to certain doors
You can throw money at me but I won't care
Negative numbers you will continue to stare
You have to manage me and kick me around
Find what the financially stable have found
Everyone is against you if you give me control
I will also put your marriage into a hole
Promises of luxury and a better life
Will cause hardship for a man and a wife
Your financial institution may be your biggest foe
As they claim there are attempts to keep rates low
Bottom line is like you they don't enjoy a financial void
They will do everything in their power to avoid
The rules will change to control your outtake
Meanwhile your intake to you will be half baked
What remains the government will
come along and pocket
They increase your taxes no matter how much you knock it
If you explain you have bills to pay they don't care
They will take more from you than what you have to bare
Life is too busy to fight them so you try to stay alive
While the entire time your financial life is in a nose dive
I am a monster that will eat you alive then tax you for dying
Take a look at your financial statements
if you think I am lying
If your bank account looks good please don't relax
They will use this reason to get "their" money back
It's all in an effort to support me and keep me around
With the right weapons I can be gagged and bound

No worries as everyday I get uglier and fatter
There appears to be no interest in addressing the latter
I plan to be around a long time as
the school systems avoid me
While the students continue to pay the institutions their fee
Broke, poor, debt, you can call me by any name
By tomorrow the minus sign will look exactly the same

Desiring Poverty

It is my desire to be in the state I am in today
Currently I blame my employer for he won't pay
Someone offered me a plan in an
effort to change my ways
They were told to go away for I have seen better days
All of my professors will help me to financial independence
Meanwhile around my financial future I will build a fence
It is better to rely on others who only use money as a theory
Some of them looking for life in a local brewery
There are books to assist and release
me from my financial hole
But it's better to watch celebrities live in a fish bowl
Woe is me for I can't pay my bills
For a solution I will turn to Capital Hill
Look at the business report the numbers are dismal
Companies are laying off this can't be for real
I rely on them to support me and my family
They don't seem to care about little old me
Now I have no job, I didn't see it coming
Several years ago things at work were humming
But I won't give a second thought about
opportunities along the way
There are always enough hours in the day to complain
On my hopes and dreams everyone else will rain
Go to school get a good job and make lots of money
Much of the list was completed, that certainly is funny
But in this land of being broke I have plenty of company
Others surround me with no idea they are not free
But it is our desire, our hope it is what we want
Our ignorance of walking around penniless we flaunt
Begging for conglomerates to take our
money doesn't make me nervous
Freely giving funds to boards who
really don't care about us

Maybe the next generation will be
different is what is rationalized
It would be fine with me if we made poverty nationalized
Certain third world counties are off to a great start
Having no money is a philosophy close to my heart
Here comes another opportunity so I better flee
My secret must be kept that I actually desire poverty

Financial Myth

It started when we were very young.
Until this day it's the same old song
Go to school and find some work
The boss man is the real jerk
But you will have money to burn
It is all according to how much you learn
When you retire you can live off Uncle Sam
He will help you when you are in a jam
Work extra time and the money will come
Make the workplace your dear old chum
At the end of the week there is great reward
Just work for others it's not very hard
But as life goes on something's not right
Your financial future is putting up a fight
Where is this extra fluff they talked about?
You don't overspend and your job has clout
Social security is flying out the window
Once you retire there will be nothing to show
The 401K has been promised and much was put in
You are relying on others not to sin
But the funds you find are a big waste
It appears the people at the top took a big taste
Relying on others may not be key
Every time you invest there is a huge fee
Rather you pay now or down the road
Someone is there to relieve your load
Especially the government, they say you make a lot
They won't allow you to give yourself a shot
Rather they want you to rely on them for comfort
Of course it is your very livelihood they will port
Realize early you have been taught a falsehood
It is only yourself that will do you good
Big banks, corporations and politicians
have there own perspective
They really don't coincide with your objective

Remember, the financial myth wasn't started by you
That's why the rich are an amazing few

Making Plans

Man without vision shall perish
Be sure to be among the rarest
People fail to plan then don't understand
Why at the end of the road life is bland
Be the chosen few to shake things up
Leave it to others if they want to pass the buck

Money Matters

Take control of me and your life will be better
If not then watch out for your debtor
A hole in the bag is what most people seek
Thinking heaven is home to the poor and the meek
If you don't control me your business will fold
You will have a zero balance until you are old
Any attempts to manipulate the market will be in vain
This will cause interest rates to drive you insane
If you try to buy low I won't be around
If you buy high you will look like a clown
Stay away from stocks you don't know what to do
The people who are in it at times are sad and blue
Over the horizon you will see the politician on the way
They say they have a plan which will surely save the day
This will return me to your hands and
business will boom again
I will be made strong and you and I will be friends
Listen to a friend's advice
Put the poor persons thought process on ice
Stop wasting time trying to punish the rich
They will escape your attacks without a hitch
The only person who will suffer is you
Remove the wealthy and your job prospects are few
Becoming rich appears to be more fun
You certainly could get a lot more done
Of course it's harder to do if I am
always going to Washington
If you and I stay together we could get more done
From the top of your head to the bottom of your shoe
If you don't control me, then I will control you
Right now me and time don't get along
Everyday it's the same old song
You need more time but don't have the money
Or you may have me which really makes it funny
Because at this point you are still in a bind

Because now you are controlled by time
The fact is, me and time get along great
It is you who has determined your own fate
For some reason you want to keep us a part
Stop giving me away to other people
is a great place to start
If you don't have me then you can't do the deed
Often the economy is fueled by greed

They will separate us if you let them
Sellers may say you can afford it over and over again
The sales pitch may be disguised in paying for it over time
The next thing you know the economy is in a bind
No one wants to let me go
Now the government starts to put on a show
At times they will be smart and cut your tax
Other times what they do gives your job the axe
Then they will go after the rich and so the story goes
I just explained what to in avoiding your foes
Stop manipulating the market you are losing time
I will come back to you, but he isn't as kind
Once he is gone he isn't coming back
Even if you have me lined up in several stacks
Take control and make no mistake
Controlling me isn't a piece of cake
Wealth is a thought process that many people lack
You must first have it before you can have those stacks
If you take money from the rich I will come around again
Once again we will be good friends
The man or woman you sent to
represent you on Capitol Hill
Do they believe wasting me is a huge thrill?
Or do they have the thought process to turn things around
You need to think rich is what the successful have found

This will help you grow into the person you were born to be
The ability to go forth and see what you can see
With the rich, I will stick to them like glue
Could you tell me why, this can't be you?

The truth about taxes

When the government needs money they come to us
They need money for the roads to run the city bus
Maybe it's to fund schools to make the children smart
Sometimes it's hard to tell the students
and politicians apart
The local including the county, state and federal are busy
They are dutifully taking money from you and me
No government program too big, no one too poor
If you give them money they will ask for more
They claim prosperity will be ours if you pay today
There is no interest in what you have to say
You may need the money for your rent
Uncle Sam says that money is already spent
We can use that money to create jobs you explain
It would be better to hand it over they exclaim
The tax won't last for long it is to get us over a hump
Ask them when the last time that was
true, the politician is stumped
They say don't worry we will tax the rich
We will then pay you, it's a perfect fit
But the rich produces jobs and now they will have less
It is unclear why the money is going to congress
If it is cheaper to manufacture overseas
the corporation will go there
Taking your job with it, not sure how this is fair
Besides that the company has now
passed the tax onto me
Meanwhile you call the increases some sort of fee
The lobbyists are in your face and you in my pocket
You take money from your constituents faster than a rocket
Government gets bigger and the dreams
of the people grow small.
It appears our elected official don't care at all
Every two to four years it is the same thing
Vote for us and we will make this country sing

Then the time comes and our money grows less
Our elected officials call the ordeal progress
They take the money then keep it as their own
Do what they say or they will take your home
No country has taxed itself into prosperity
Yet everyday we pay into this so called fee
It is the truth and one day it must change
The entire structure itself must be rearranged

SPEAKING
OF
SELFHELP

21 Days

Mistakes from the past can be erased pretty fast
Doing the same thing again keeps the past
There is a strategy to make some improvements
One day others will wonder where the negative went
Discipline will keep you on track
You can change your ways and keep the facts
You have the ability if you possess the will
Knowing what it takes to fit the bill
It just takes 21 days to make a change
This timeframe keeps your goal in range
If there is something you want to make happen
Go ahead and set yourself up for the win
Remember what you have to say
Go ahead and make your decision today

Alcohol

I love you and call you friend
You will be with me until the end
When I was failing classes and feeling down
You helped me finals week to come around
This time period I will not fester
After all there is always next semester
After class we went out on a night on the town
Surveying our group you couldn't tell the bigger clown
The girl everyone thought looked like a mule
After a few drinks it turns out they were the fool
The frat parties, the bars it was all a good time
After a great night out me and the gang felt just fine
But others have fallen to your allure and temptation
You have caused certain organizations much frustration
Lives have been lost either instantly or slow marination
Such destructive behavior has existed since your creation
They tried prohibition but the product was still sold
Today the argument of your removal is just plain old
Your presence to people is as good as gold
Many will sacrifice their career, homes
or loved ones for a drink
One should stop, look around before
telling others what to think
The harm that is caused often cannot be reversed
Especially when your victims are carted off
in a hearse
When you see certain ads they never
talk about the consequence
Only the good times that is had in a
very positive circumstance
Perhaps the blame should fall on the customer
The reason the night before is one big blur
Saying you are sorry may not remove all of the pain
The reason behind your actions will be seen as lame

Although alcohol may claim to be your friend in the end
The reason for that end may be due to your friend

Association

Hang around those people you will be just like them
Just look at where they have been
Then look forward and see what's ahead
What's around you may not be positive I'm afraid
If your associates are positive then that's good
This will help accelerate you to a better neighborhood
If they are negative, you will find out what it means
The r is removed and you will find out the fiends
They say they are your friend and they mean well
Often their ways are a very soft sell
Everything is great and you are doing fine
Often many people here the exact same line
You may live your life and think it's fun
You can't run with the skunks and not smell like one

Authentic manhood

The makings of a man start when he is a very small boy
A lot can be seen during downtime
when he plays with his toy
As he gets older life and responsibility begin to take toll
Often it is challenging for the male to find his role
If he grew up as part of a nuclear family
he can look to Dad as a guide
Some of the surveys blame single mom
because his grades would slide
He grows up the holidays roll around
He doesn't notice his new bride wears a frown
Mom is inviting her son to spend the holiday with her
Without thinking the new groom does concur
Much later he learns his family has changed
The lesson here is that his life has been rearranged
The life as a boy has been set aside
It is with this new woman he must confide
Life lessons are better learned even if they are learned late
When accepting invitations from the
old life the man should hesitate
Hanging out with the boys and not moving forward
This kind of behavior can make the
new family life awkward
Family life is the most important structure around
It formulates the other structures to help make them sound
The man must set an example for the
rest of the family to follow
Acting like that once small child will make
it difficult for others to swallow
They say the apple doesn't fall too far from the tree
That's why the man should be all he can be
Love his family and give his all to the community
Because it is that love and dedication that others must see
The new generation may make fun of old traditional values
But it's important the family stick together like glue

The man keeps it together for he is the eye of the storm
Of course with the aid of his lovely
assistant attached to his arm

Cease the day

Every day is a time of opportunity
Taking advantage of it is key
Tomorrow is not promised
Yesterday is missed
Live for the moment
Before you are dismissed

Chances

There are people we know, but many
others we don't have their name
As we go through life many of us don't
care about them just the same
The cosmos of life can be complicated
and extremely delicate
It's possible the outcome of someone
else depends on our etiquette
For instance, if you offer a friendly hello it just may fit
If you don't it may throw everything
into frenzy and start a chain
At the end of the day no one would be
the wiser that you were the blame
Taking a few minutes to help that person
or offer a friendly greeting
May have made the difference if that person
were to receive a severe beating
Perhaps on a positive note that person you just brushed by
Could be someone who could help you
with your woes, a very intelligent guy
Or it could be the designer to your next house,
or more personal your next spouse
Maybe you are single for a reason, perhaps
you ran by your spouse last season
There is the likelihood that Karma wants to talk to you
About how the past few years you have
made those around you quite blue
Chances are your time has come and
the evidence may be very clear
You may have been the manager where
your subordinates' quit due to fear
Or the husband who cheated on his dedicated
wife while she cared for the home
Being a more public figure you could have
abused your time on the microphone

Rather you have been a bad boss, terrible
husband, bad wife or abusive star
Chances are you are the reason you are where you are
But in the grand scheme of things you
may have affected others as well
Perhaps not knowing exactly where your
cards or the other persons deck fell
Now you have the information and
by now there is no doubt
That you are better off in life if you just help others out
Increase your chances in making this earth a better place
By helping others succeed in what we call the human race

Change

Change will do you good, once the concept is understood
Some cases require you change your entire neighborhood
Other alterations require you change
your skill set if you could
It doesn't matter what you do it won't remain the same
At times you will sit around wondering who to blame
Sometimes things are better left alone
as you keep on your path
Amazingly unwittingly you are forced
to cut your budget in half
Trying to make things better you may
in fact make them worst
Doing this on a consistent basis you
may think you are cursed
Your life may be rearranged without
others telling you its coming
This you don't understand because up to
this point things were humming
Now you are forced to relocate or just plain vacate
This entire ordeal is putting a lot on your plate
You may feel you can't take this any longer
It's times like this that makes a person stronger
Chances are you don't want to learn anything new today
Or hear what anyone else has to say
However, going forward is something you do anyway
It's a game of odds and sometimes
you can move it in your favor
Early on in the game it helps to pick your flavor
With power you have many more
options in which to choose
Play your cards right and in many cases you just can't lose
If you trust a person who will remove the
status quo there may be a Shock
This sort of behavior continues around the clock

You may prefer a Laissez-faire attitude
when it comes to your own affairs
Make your own decisions early if you dare
If you find you are wrong then attempt to rearrange
The only thing constant in life of course, is change

Character

It is what many people prefer
Better situations will occur
In this philosophy we should feed
We need this person to lead
If you think it doesn't matter
Later you may concur
Once this person is in control
You will quickly learn of their role
Often the reflection may be on you
Perhaps you should change your view
Its better that you prefer
That the quality you seek is character

Encouragement

So much of it is lost
Little is provided by your boss
Studies have shown encouragement is a motivator
The opposite occurs with a designated eliminator
A writer wasn't sure of the future
Showing others his work was torture
During the middle of the night his transcript was mailed
He didn't want others to know if he failed
His transcript wasn't widely received
Yet later accolade he did achieve
His works although he wasn't paid
It served as a life long aid
This writer gained fame and success
Through out his life he did his very best
Now others have benefited from one single act
His works are very famous, now that's a fact
There may be someone in your ranks who needs you
Your kind words of encouragement may add great value
Take your eyes off yourself and make a difference
That person may need you as a positive reference
We are surrounded by people of great wisdom
Recognizing them may be seldom
Eventually these individuals will pull
themselves through the ranks
They will accept their reward and give thanks
They will explain how much you meant
That day you offered them encouragement

Enthusiasm

Your excitement can make a huge difference
Showing you believe will persuade others by your inference
If you believe odds are your philosophy they will swallow
Go ahead be a leader and others will follow
Everyone has their own opinion this is true
Believe in yourself and they will believe in you
The more you fail the bigger your success
Without failure there would be no progress
Even people on the top of world wish to improve
Watch as they plot and plan their very next move
The merchant doesn't stop at one store he may build more
The winner will tally his loses as he works to rebuild his score
He will acknowledge his shortcomings until there are few
This will improve his enthusiasm as he talks to you
When he speaks you will know he is going places
Just take a look at the expression on his followers' faces
Success will be placed in the appropriate format
As his dreams and goals are laid neatly under his hat
Just look at the joy a belief can bring
When you're excited you don't have
to worry about trivial things

Failure

You are constantly in need of my assistance
Despite your desire to abolish my existence
Denial is what you embrace when I come along
Admittedly, this attitude really is not wrong
Today I am only here to point out
What my true existence is all about
The concern comes about when you keep me around
When my true meaning is never found
I am here to make sure you do your best
To find the true meaning of success
Without me, your potential would be lost
You would not learn to be your own boss
If you see others fail, it should help you learn
This is important since you do not have time to burn
Life is short and not all failure will be done by you
At the same time, you will have plenty to choose
There are times you will and wish me away
Keep your endurance, you will be OK.
Believe in yourself and trust the right people
If you don't you will die weak and feeble
Without my frequent visit, you won't know achievement
Most importantly, success is heaven sent
Many of your greatest achievers saw a lot of me
They are among the biggest failures you ever did see
Historically you will read about how well they did
Often it isn't mentioned how previously they lost the bid
What is discussed is the influence over our nation
What's forgotten is the constant frustration
However, don't worry I am here to remind you
Without me, you don't have a clue.

Faith

If you have it you can do wonders with your life
It can help you when you are going
through turmoil and strife
Often you can't see or hear but just sense it is there
Materialization is often not an option even if you stare
If you are going through a tough time
just remember the name
Because sometimes life can play a
series of very harsh games
Others may question your motives and
you will have nothing to show them
Trying to deal with these individuals and
turn them around may be slim
Knowing the truth however is at your
fingertips and within reach
Don't deny your belief for doing so
would be your security breach
Look around there are others who will
guide you to the correct place
Ironically your belief is written all over your face
Listening to others may be easier to do
because there are so many
Critics and non-believers are constantly in
your path because there are plenty
Just when times are tough signs will arise
where at first you won't recognize
Others missed these markings
unfortunately it lead to their demise
But not you because you have the
faith to move full speed ahead
Although there are some days that
approach which you surly dread
Faith isn't made easy because it is not
for the doubters or the weak

You can obtain Faith even if you are
misguided or even meek
The light is shown through Faith and
she is often misunderstood
Mainly because she isn't found living walking
aimlessly though your neighborhood
She is in you and a part of you as you begin
to acknowledge the realization
That having Faith may require opening your
eyes and having the dedication
Finding Faith isn't always easy but once she
arrives try not to loose what you have
It may be challenging because others may
protest or just poke fun and laugh
Knowing in the end you will be right
may help just a little
However, for others there may not be an acquittal
Life will make you jump though hoops
and make you wonder why
Sometimes on really bad days you will
want to break down and cry
Just keep her by your side or in your heart
and you will find the reward is great
Of course this will all be determined as
life finally acknowledges your fate
Without you there can be no tomorrow
for you must believe something
Otherwise your life has no beginning
or end but a continuous ring
If you don't stand for something
you will fall for anything
Living life in a circle is no way to live
When you believe give all you can give
you only get one chance, don't treat life as a fling
Because when the song is over you can no longer sing
Believe in yourself and others will follow
No one wants to listen to someone who is shallow

One syllable will assist you in being safe
Just remember to keep your Faith

Gangster Love

Keeping your people together is a great start
Today you put a bullet through your brother's heart
He was not part of your group now he is dead
He wasn't from around here which made you afraid
You have your own rules which you want others to follow
Not once did you stop and think that your laws are shallow
Others may not be aware what your colors may mean
Your lifestyle is a road to nowhere it may seem
How many had to die because you
said they did not respect
For this you put bullets inside people without any regret
The young man you shot was headed for a better situation
He was preparing for college in an
effort to further his education
He was sitting with his classmate having
lunch and enjoying his day
A visit from a stranger asked a question
but didn't like what he had to say
Responding where he was from is
the honest answer he gave
Not knowing his response would soon land him in his grave
Shortly others came after that response
in the middle of the café
A hail of bullets rang out in the middle of the day
Our agenda is what is important and it
doesn't matter who gets hurt
Another human will get shot if we
don't like the color of his shirt
It's all about code and honor you wouldn't understand .
Our goal is to spread our ignorance
throughout the entire land
If your son or daughter feels they need
a family we have one here
We are here to protect them, they should have no fear

If someone tries to harm them we
will stab them in the heart
Now that is a fine place to start

Getting there

People often think if they could get out of
their current situation life would improve
Whether it is changing their way of life
or making another type of move
If you could just move forward and get out of here
Once this move is made you will have nothing to fear
Currently, life just isn't fair
If I could just make it to there
It's almost as if "there" is a permanent destination
This illusion of security is the reason for the fascination
The single guy is lonely and wants a companion
He comes riding in like a very confident stallion
She thinks if I just get married life will be grand
The two get married and later she takes a stand
She proposes to continue the fascination
Life would be better if there was an additional creation
He agrees and so the story goes
Life becomes even more challenging and it shows
Get the baby out of diapers then there will be peace
Right now with this juggling act life is a real beast
Once the child is a teenager this will certainly help
They will assist this family and their
motivation will be heart felt
The child is a teenager and you don't know
what to think
They say the parents don't know
anything and they know it all
If they could get past this point, life would be a ball
Now they are in their 20's and I can see the end
Let's get them out of the house, to
higher learning we will send
Meanwhile the offspring has thoughts of his own
If I can find someone to love me my life
won't be blown

We will get married and I will be complete
Then I will have the world at my feet

Infidelity

If my spouse doesn't know, no one gets hurt.
There is no harm with a simple little flirt
It's my at work husband or wife
It's like having a double life
I will tell that person things I don't tell him
We make references to the lights going dim
Other workers are afraid to come near
It's like they have an invisible fear
It must be the inside jokes we share
Sometimes our humor is hard to bear
They just don't understand you are my friend
You will be there until the very end
Let's go for drinks to celebrate our fun
We will retire to my place when we are done
The wife is away and she won't mind
It's not often with this type of friendship you find
The husband is away on business but I will be sure to call
To assure him there is no threat to our relationship at all
Later that night the tide began to turn
I felt the urge inside of me begin to burn
The look in your eyes should have been no surprise
We were together until sunrise
Time to go, we must head to work
If my husband finds out he will go berzerk
Better he doesn't find out, he won't understand
We didn't know infidelity was in the plan
Back to work that day and no one knows the difference
Of course our relationship makes perfect sense
Lately the biggest fear isn't my spouse
Rather that our relationship will go south
Then the workplace will be a disaster
It may impede the promotion I am after
We have seen others actually lose their job
In an instant their career was robbed

But it must be worth it because we continue to frolic
Making some of our coworkers literally sick
Understanding of course it is all in fun
Our lives as friends has only just begun

Inspiration

My present is used to remember my past
Often it feels my future is moving very fast
Tomorrow is not promised but yesterday is clear
Living for tomorrow should not be done out of fear
Utilize your experience to assist someone else
As today goes by don't just think of yourself
You have the power to inspire and make things better
Currently, you have your future down to the letter
As you live life remember it is not forever
Use this time to make your environment better
You have the power to mold, lead and inspire
Your love and hope can be used for others to acquire

It's a man's world

Take a look around and what do you see
The male taking control of you and me
Before he wanted the woman quiet and submissive
Put an idea on the table and his attitude
was dismissive
But in the midst the woman did great things
This in addition to the love she often brings
The inspiration she provides to make
the world better
She is sweet, kind hearted and extremely clever
But when it comes to National Security
The man is often left in charge to pull the lever
There may have been a challenge he
would be removed from the fold
There was that time he didn't want
her anywhere near the poll
Moving forward the woman took more control
Maybe man is upset about what
happen in the Garden of Eden
Still blaming the woman until Jesus comes again
Looking around you see the female doing more everyday
Through electronic communication you
also hear what she has to say
However in many areas the man does
not wish to give up the throne
Sometimes you will hear him remark
he wants her to stay home
Instinctively she knows how to turn a wrong
into a right.
She was the inspiration for man's first
airplane flight
On creativity she does not lag
She designed our American Flag
As time goes on the man slowly steps aside
Secretly it is the woman in whom he confides

Slowly he is listening to the nation Battle cry
Step aside, and give the woman a try

Leadership

A great leader will find
Sometimes it's necessary to leave quitters behind
He will lead and the rest will follow
She will make sure those who surround are not shallow
The traits of a leader are easy to spot
Someone who constantly talks; a leader is not
He is someone who listens to others concerns
It is your life a caring person will learn
Remember enthusiasm will help win the prize
Others will see the confidence in a leader's eyes
He realizes his mistakes and finds them early
With your shortcoming he will keep the information blurry
It is better to be diplomatic when conducting a search
If your follower is an all around sinner
have them handle it in church
Great leaders are a minority among the pack
They teach themselves this quality, that's a fact
They may not appear like one today
In this area their leadership may be grey
Be mindful there are others where
the leader can get advice
Such knowledge may keep them off thin ice
Find reasons for people to do what
they wouldn't normally do
This person can put the situation on the other shoe
Most importantly a leader can't do it without you
His followers maybe large or they may be few
At the end of the day your attitude must allow
Or the leader will have no one who will follow

Materials of Life

Life is one big juggling act
Our schedules are often packed
How you weigh things makes the difference
Think for a moment, if this isn't making sense.
Work, family, religion, finance
Now let's take a quick glance
Something to consider during your dance
Let's say the last three are made of glass
Keep in mind, the dance moves you very fast
They may fall and shatter no matter what the shape
Your daily decisions will determine your fate
Let's say work begins to fall
It will bounce back like a rubber ball
But the others may experience a dent or a knick
Sometimes beyond the point where it can be fixed
Think about where you placed your importance
Looking back would you keep the same stance?
What if you had the opportunity to order a repair?
Try swapping out the first option if you dare
The first is rubber it will bounce back
Yet we tend to put the others under attack
You have the means to adjust number four with your mind
Just leave the hourly thought process behind
There's the matter of letting religion go astray
Of course there is that small reminder
regarding Judgment Day
It all started with the family where your values
were placed
Unless that glass structure was shattered all over
the place
The opportunity to make it right is now
Think about the type of material
before you make your vow

What may appear important may
actually be your downfall
You only have one life to live after all

Negative People

They will bring you down when you are up
They will be there to keep you down on your luck
Not an encouraging word they will speak
They will continue to tell you your life is bleak
You may spend your life not knowing the difference
To you, everything they do may make sense
During your life they will conveniently blend
Calling themselves your closest of friend
Take the time to weed them out
You will know because they will immediately pout
Since their own life is down in the dumps
They don't want to see you get over your humps
Misery loves company and has a high popularity rate
Don't let the majority of evil determine your fate
Throw those people overboard and leave them alone
Soon the belly of a whale will be their new home
Your waters will be less rough
Life itself won't be as tough
Sadly, people don't want to see you move ahead
Many of your associates are mentally dead
Most are dead by age 24
Sadly they aren't buried until 74
Raise yourself above and be a positive influence
You can do it, if all of this actually makes sense

Procrastination

There is no hurry when you have me on your side
No need to do your homework just let it slide
The big project you have for work can certainly wait
Spend time away from what is due,
in this case don't hesitate
Those who defy me find themselves in the arena of winners
The devil will house them as his group of sinners
Because a rocket ship on your back
will propel you to success
You will go on to riches on earth and
beyond as you are blessed
But if you listen to me your responsibility will be few
Your free time will stick to you as if it were glue
If you look at all the successful people of the land
Many of them were productive as
they draw a line in the sand
Satan had a meeting one day as he
watched too many go forward
He said if too many people keep this
up they will see the Lord
His group of advisors was called to come up with a plan
They watched at the round table as
he buried his face in his hands
One by one they came up with a suggestion
on how to slow people down
Each advisor watched as the devil continued his frown
Then a special guest arrived on the bottom floor
Send him in Lucifer shouted! There must be more
Introduce yourself then tell me your idea
Because my Kingdom currently is in fear
No need to worry for I am clearly relaxed
With humans it is easy to explain the facts
I rule the household, workplace and people with flare
Dangers of other diseases do not compare
I will lower your grades and separate your family

You will never achieve financial inherence with my fee
With my plan you will lose site of your
goals by watching others
You will lack motivation for your future I will smother
My disease is spread throughout the nation
You may know me more formally as Procrastination.

Racism in America

Others are not treated fairly or maybe
you are guilty of it too
Different ways of spreading negative
as you share your point of view.
Blame it on the past you may hear others tout
Today we will not hire you because we have the clout
Your family lives in a certain neighborhood because of your color
Or maybe you have a very low credit score like no other
Again you look to the past to answer your woes of today
Thinking maybe it's possible you live in
that area because you are gay
Whatever the reason of course we can't erase the past
Many different forms of discrimination exist in every class
Looking ahead it's quite possible
everyone isn't out to get you
Not getting that position could be
because you don't have a clue
The employer says he wanted to hire you
in part to satisfy the special interest
But at the end of the day many saw the axe
as they lost their hard earned nest
The proper credentials are needed to
work legally in this fine land
Breaking the law and calling it racism doesn't make things grand
Since you are looking at history take a look
at those who did it on their own
Many paved their own way instead of
waiting to be someone's clone
Of course there is an existence of ugly hate and despair
Be part of the solution as others stop and stare
At the end of our time on this earth here is the real twist
Sometimes we find racism even when none exist

Rumors

As humans it must be reported what is said
Information is processed until the person is dead
The story will be repeated in all its glory
Never letting the facts get in the way of a good story
Socrates had a different take to keep his pride
He would ask if the information was verified.
How good is the information was asked of the student?
His response was the news was quite bent
It's part of a three part test
It is to bring about the very best
If the rule is applied
The Rumors can be denied
The final question that can be asked
Before the information is passed along too fast
Finally, let's put the situation on the other shoe
Does what you have to say provide value?
"No" is what you have to say.
Then the best thing is to put the rumor away

Status

It's called status, and its for stupid people
Working day after day makes you weak and feeble
You want to drive a certain car and
live in a certain area code
Because of this your life carries a very heavy load
Keeping up with the Joneses is the life you seek
Never stopping to think to them life is also bleak
10 feet forward and 10 feet back
This is how you will live your life, that's a fact
If you don't train your brain different it will be the same
If you think this isn't true, then you are insane
98% of America is on the fast track to failure
Be among the 2% who has found the cure
Concentrate on your own goals and belief
Otherwise life will present a multitude of grief

Struggles of the Philanderer

Today my desires I shall feed
As I take advantage of someone else's needs
When the time came, we had no regret
It was at that moment our greatest fear was met
As I hurried & ran out the back door
That's when the mad man called his woman a whore
Then I sped off in my shiny new ride
I thought of myself with great pride
There is one decision I should probably make
The next step I will defiantly take
The solution is easy what the heck?
Stay away from women with husbands with no neck
Be sure the husband is skinny and cannot fight
This will make the situation quite light
During my reflection, I realize what life is about
Make sure when you sin, that no one finds out

The Criminal Mind

When you commit the crime you get mad at the police. Understand as long as you are a criminal, you have no peace

The Guardrails

The Lord has 10 Commandments on how you should live
They are not suggestions or do what you think you feel
He is commanding you to do his will
Think of guardrails on a bridge or overpass
If you defy them it could be your last
If you walk along the bridge you are on his trail
You know this is correct because the devil is on your tail
You may reach outside the rail to
pursue lust, money or fame
Then you find yourself falling into
danger as you point blame
As time goes on the pace becomes very fast
Yet you see your friends and neighbors' fall past
Then you realize two angels are lifting you toward victory
You don't understand what happened
because death is the fee
The wages of sin is death
It's better to arrive in heaven with poor health
But in this case your soul is spared
As your book of life is shared
You walked in the path of rightness
While the devil looked on in disgust
He is angry today because he has lost another
But he quickly turns his attention toward your brother
There are many who ignore the guardrails altogether
Taking their souls is easy as lifting a feather
It is the challenges for Satan where he doesn't want to fail
Because when life is over he wants to put you in a fiery jail
He stands outside the guardrails inviting you to take part
Saying whatever he can to win your heart
But if you keep the devil on the other side of the guardrail
His evil versus the love of Jesus will pail

Trust

Wouldn't it be great if we could go
through life without worries?
If everyone was as pure as the whitest snow flurry
There would be no prison or even a jail
No bother with a place known as hell
Think of it and all of the joy this would bring
You wouldn't have to worry about a thing
Voting for your favorite candidate there would be no fear
Because you know in the correct
direction this person would steer
No Weapons of Mass Destruction would be found
Because on the platform of life foreign
leaders would stand their ground
On a more general front if a stranger needed a ride
You could pick them up without breaking your stride
Because you know that person needed what they say
That they actually needed your help today
A deposit at the bank needs to be made
Let's stop this perfect stranger before the day is to fade
Since that person is going that way
it will just be a second more
This way more time is spent with the
family with whom we adore
These concepts which are brought
before you may seem unreal
For a lifestyle of this magnitude it's difficult to get a feel
But think of it in its most pure form
No one would know different if it were this
way since the day you were born
Much stress would be eliminated for
every parent who raised a child
The conflict between a teenager and
authority would be quite mild
At this point it would take a miracle
to make the adjustment

We just need for you and your neighbor to take a hint
We are all that we have and without
the other no one survives
At some point trust must be used or
individually we take a nose dive
The Captain of a plane or the engineer of your car
We trust these people to take us far
Even if you choose to spend the rest of your life walking
Or speaking only to yourself as you proceed in talking
This would only make sense since the beginning is clear
It is in yourself you must trust in order to get it in first gear

When I see you smile

When I look at you, I see you look at me
Your eyes as pretty and bright as can be
I am not sure what I did to deserve you
A person of your caliber, there are only a few
The other person your dad says gave you birth
Yet I am convinced there is no one like you on this earth
When I see you smile I can face anything
There is nothing like the happiness and joy you bring
When you look at me I see nothing but love
Caring and nurturing sent directly from above
Life with you is certainly the perfect ride
That is why you are my lovely bride
It is apparent others would see the glory I see
When I see you smile it's a love meant to be
It's amazing how I got to you first
With your love for me I am well versed
Take it from a pro who knows heart ache well
I am deeply in love with you, can't you tell?

Winners Philosophy

The Philosophy of a winner can turn a zero into a hero
Mentality and association will assist with this flow
Bringing others along is a bigger achievement
As you get older you will wonder where the time went
If you are a loser please step aside
It is not good to bring you along for the ride
A loser will attempt to slow you down
Darkening your day with his continuous frown
Hopes, dreams, and aspirations is the key
Often it's achieved when I don't focus on me
Most of your stories of success are achieved by looking out
This is what living life as a winner is all about.
Often a loser can't stay with me long
He will make excuses as he is proven wrong
Excuses are for the weak and incompetent
At wartime only the strong should be sent
The loser's job is to sit around and complain
Explain to nearby listeners others are to blame
Winners understand hard times will come to past
Historically you will find it did not last
A winner will find ways to get it done
The loser will think of every excuse under the sun
Once you decide what you are going to do
The goal that you set shall ring true
Join the circle of winners you will find the association great
You will be on the other side of winning if you hesitate
The key to success is simple you know
That's making sure your efforts are not for show
If you follow these guidelines you certainly will be cooking
Character is who you are when no one else is looking
Really helping others to keep their life in tact
Will ensure in the view of others you are a class act

Without you

You came and kept things in perspective
Your decision was truly an elective
Good things come to those who wait
Luckily, for us you did not hesitate
The burden on your shoulders were heavy
Observers however explained you as quite merry
As you went through life to help those, you love
As if you were personally sent from the man above
To you your actions may appear quite ordinary
However, to insiders the situation is quite the contrary
Thank you for being the person you are
Creating a role model for those near and far
If scientists could figure out a way to duplicate you
The world's problems would be very few

You and I

You and I is all I need
I want you for myself I plead
You are so very beautiful I can't describe
Emotionally my heart was offered a bribe
It was accepted I am afraid to say
Love is scary, but I want you anyway
When I look at you my heart stops
Time stands still along with the clock
It started off as a simple flirt
Sometimes I wonder if I will get hurt
But at this hour I shall not worry
As my logic grows more blurry
You are all I need to make the world better
You have my love, down to the letter

www.ingramcontent.com/pod-product-compliance
Lightning Source LLC
LaVergne TN
LVHW041627070426
835507LV00008B/488